AFFIRMATIONS FOR SELF ESTEEM DEVELOPMENT

AFFIRMATIONS FOR SELF ESTEEM DEVELOPMENT

LIFE SERIES VOL. 1

NORA M. HUDSON

authorHOUSE®

AuthorHouse™
1663 Liberty Drive
Bloomington, IN 47403
www.authorhouse.com
Phone: 1-800-839-8640

Published by AuthorHouse   03/27/2013

ISBN: 978-1-4817-0140-2 (sc)

A GLANCE IN THE MIRROR
A STRANGERS FACE.
EYES BELONGING TO MY MOTHER.
LIPS BELONGING TO MY FATHER
NOSE PUGGED/SQUARE/SHARP OR
FINE?
A HAUNTED LONGING TO KNOW......
WHO?
EVEN WHEN ?WHERE? OR HOW?
I NEED TO TOUCH AND FEEL
TO KNOW THE SUBSTANCE OF
THAT SOUL
AN UNASKED QUESTION
A MYSTERY WITH NO TEACHER
TWISTED, TURNED, and shown
my fate???????/

*I GLANCE IN THE MIRROR....DO I
SEE ?????????????*

This book consists of three
(3) phases of development.
The first is the affirmation
phase. This phase allows the
reader to begin to program
their thinking in a positive
way.

   The second phase happens
outside of this book. It
is the practice of loving
yourself and teaching
yourself when faced with
self judgment to chose love
and peace.

   The third and final phase
is the journaling phase
which I hope will continue

and stay with you for a lifetime. It allows you to reflect on who, and what you are.

This journey to self knowledge and love is a wonderful journey. It is the journey of life . It will involve you and others. It will help you stay in the present. It will keep you grounded. Be assured that there will be tears, remorse, joy and even some strain but know that the finished product will be ready to press forward into the self actualizing person you were created to be.

Journal Activity

The journal activity section is used to allow you to understand the importance of focusing and writing your experiences. Use these journaling activities to look inside yourself, your heart, your mind.

I would advise that you complete your journaling activity in the evening. You will have had the opportunity to live and practice the affirmation. What were your barriers to the affirmation? What positive situations or circumstances developed out

of your daily affirmations.
For best results try to
stay away from yes, no or
one word answers to the
questions. Feel free to
let your feelings flow.
Open your daily journal
and describe how you are
feeling. Just talk to
yourself.

There are no right or wrong
answers as each persons
experiences, feelings,
reactions will be different.
This is your time to
honestly be you.

<u>Affirmations</u>

Affirmations are merely words strung together to form an idea which you give meaning to. These affirmations are simplistic in content, geared solely for the purpose of self talk, exploration and development.

To be most effective the affirmations should be used in conjunction with the Self affirming activity as this will allow you to do self exploration and appraisal.

THE FIRST FOUR AFFIRMATIONS ARE TO BE READ, MEMORIZED AND REPEATED EACH DAY.

Start by selecting a certain time in the morning to read the affirmation. This will allow you to practice and live the affirmation for the whole day.

Begin by reading the affirmation to yourself.

Look in the mirror and read the affirmation again. This time with feeling.

Think about how it applies to you?

Question yourself? Am I living by these words? Challenge yourself ,what do I need to do so that I can incorporate these affirmations into my life?

Write the affirmation either in the journaling section of this manual or in a notebook/calendar or slip of paper. Read the affirmation during the day. The purpose is to allow you to retain the affirmation.

foreword

There is a general assumption that certain traits like self love or self esteem naturally occur in humans unless there has been some traumatic event to interfere with the natural development. It is my belief that self love and self esteem are developmental milestones which must be cultivated and refined like any other talent.

There has been a great focus on affirmations as a way of changing or modeling behavior in adults. How much farther ahead would we be if we focused upon developing positive self esteem in the formative years of our life.

This life series- volume 1 contains three written division although there has been a fourth division mentioned. The second dimension is the actualization of this process.

Make a daily commitment to read the affirmation. Live the affirmation

And journal for best results.

There is only one rule. "Everything you write must direct itself to positive thinking." For example if you were to have an experience where you believed someone made you feel less than special. It is okay to write that someone made you feel less than special but you must replace that thought with a positive, both mentally and in writing.

This manual is about empowering the positive within us

This manual is about overcoming everything that is not positive

GETTING STARTED.

TOOLS NEEDED.
MIRROR
PENCILS/PENS/MARKERS
THIS MANUAL FOR SELF ESTEEM
    DEVELOPMENT
A PERSONAL COMMITMENT TO COMPLETE
    ALLL ASSIGNMMENTS.
AN UNDERSTANDING THAT IF YOU:
A. APPROACH THESE AFFIRMATIONS AS
A CULTIVATING AND REFINING PROCESS
WHICH GIVES YOU THE OPPURTUNITY FOR
PERSONAL GROWTH.

B. YOU WILL BE ABLE TO LOOK YOURSELF
IN YOUR OWN EYES AND SAY YOU
LOVE YOURSELF WITHOUT JUDGMENT
OR HESITATION..YOU HAVE THEN
INTERNALIZED AND INTEGRATED THE
AFFIRMATIONS IN YOUR LIFE.
C. KNOW THAT THE ONY PERSON WHO CAN
GUAGE/MEASURE YOU IS YOU!

D. WHEN YOU LOOK YOURSELF IN THE EYE
AND SAY,"I LOVE MYSELF ..I am wonderful
the little voice in you should be agreeing. If

the little voice finds reason to say you are unworthy use the affirmation to overcome the voice. The little voice within may even point to specific examples as to why you are unworthy love......but this is a process of replacing old thoughts with new thoughts ..you can and will overcome the negative.

E. in spite of all the little voice says... you say your affirmation loud...louder ..I love myself ..I am wonderful ..I am worthy!!!!

F. you have succeeded the day you say I love myself and the little voice agrees ..yes you do love yourself and you are worthy of love...then

1. Live like you love yourself!
2. Act like you love yourself!
3. treat yourself like you love yourself.

<u>*The Beginning*</u>

TURN TO AFFIRMATION 1.
STAND IN FRONT OF YOUR MIRROR AND
LOOK YOURSELF IN THE EYE AND SAY THE
AFFIRMATION LOUD.
THINK ABOUT HOW YOU ARE FEELING
WHEN YOU SAY THE AFFIRMATION? How
do you feel when you look yourself in the
eye?
Repeat the affirmation. Does it make
the affirmation more real to you? Does it
energize you? Can you say with conviction
yes after you have read the affirmation?
Write the affirmation in a calendar/notebook
or on a slip of paper which you should carry
with you at all times and read it several
times during the day.
Read affirmation #2
Think about how you feel about yourself
and what you are doing. Are you present
and attending. (Being present means you
are being focused and attending means as
a participant attempting to integrate this
affirmation in your life.)
Reread the affirmation @2 even if you do not
feel compelled to take action you should

begin to at least ask yourself questions about your relationship with yourself.

<u>Read affirmation #3</u>

Think about how it feels.

How are you feeling?

What does it make you think about?

Read/write/recite affirmations #1 and #2 and #3 in order.

<u>Read affirmation #4</u>

Do you feel more comfortable with yourself. Read/write/recite affirmations #1,#2,#3,#4. You should have a slip of paper which after the 4th day will always have five (5) affirmations on them. The first four affirmations are geared toward self exploration as well as allowing you to become comfortable with yourself. These affirmations are the building blocks for integration and internalization of the other affirmations. As you begin this committed venture I pray that you are able to know, love, and appreciate how special you are.

My name is _____

"I AM COMMITTED TO BEING THE BEST I CAN BE!!!!!!!! I AM WONDERFUL!! I WAS BORN TO BE SUCCESSFUL AND SPIRITUAL!!!!!!!!!!!! I AM SELF MOTIVATED AND I MUST BEGIN THE PROCESS OF REFINING ALL THAT I AM!!!!!!!"

"I will love myself *unconditionally, and focus on the good that is happening to me!!!!!!!!!!!!!!!!!!!"

* unconditionally means without judgment reservation or hesitation

Affirmation #3
(recite this affirmation daily)

"I WILL SMILE AT MYSELF AND MEAN IT!!!"

1. YOU MUST USE A MIRROR. LOOK YOURSELF IN THE EYE FOR THIRTY SECONDS.

2. TIE A STRING AROUND YOUR FINGER OR USE A RING. Each time you look at the string/ring smile at yourself.

3. Do this everyday

Affirmation #4
(Do this affirmation daily)

'I WILL HUG MYSELF TO DEMONSTRATE LOVE FOR MYSELF!!!'

1. WHILE YOU ARE AT THE MIRROR SMILING AT YOURSELF. Wrap your arms around yourself and hug yourself two or three times

2. Do this everyday...and as often as you do it "smile" at yourself.

AFFIRMATION #5

"I WILL DO *SOMETHING* *SPECIAL* FOR MYSELF TODAY.!"

I WILL WRITE DOWN WHAT I WILL DO SPECIAL FOR MYSELF TODAY AND PUT IT IN MY POCKET.

"I AM THANKFUL FOR ALL THAT I AM AND ALL THAT I HAVE AND AM WORKING TOWARD THAT WHICH I WANT"

"I CAN DO ALL THAT I WANT TO DO.... AS LONG AS I KNOW WHAT I WANT TO DO.!!!"

"I AM BEING THE BEST I CAN BE IN ALL I DO TODAY!!"

"TODAY I WILL SHARE MYSELF BY SMILING AT EVERYONE I MEET!!!"

"I AM ONLY USING GOOD AND POSITIVE SELF TALK TODAY!!"

"POSITIVE THOUGHTS GROW FROM POSITIVE ACTIONS!!"

AFFIRMATION #12

"I AM MOLDING MY PRESENT TO THE SHAPE OF MY FUTURE!!"

AFFIRMATION #13

"I DO NOT BEAT MYSELF

FOR MY PAST..I

EMPOWER

MYSELF FOR

MY

FUTURE!!!"

"I ACCEPT COMPLIMENTS WITH A SMILE.. I AM PROUD OF MY ACCOMPLISHMENTS..I DO NOT HIDE MY TALLENTS UNDER A BASKET!!"

"CRITICISM IS A TOOL FOR BECOMING A BETTER PERSON.... IT IS NOT A REFLECTION OF WHO I AM!!"

"LOVING MYSELF IS NECESSARY BEFORE I CAN GIVE OR RECEIVE LOVE.

The gift of LOVE is the greatest gift of all!!!"

"I HAVE *CONFIDENCE* IN MYSELF. I AM PROUD OF WHO I AM!!!"

AFFIRMATION #18

"I LOOK INSIDE MYSELF TO UNCOVER MY UNIQUE TALENTS AND GIFTS!!!"

"I AM DETERMINED TO SUCCEED IN ALL THAT I DO... I PUT FORTH EFFORT...TIME.. AND CONCENTRATION!

"I KNOW MY HISTORY...I ACKNOWLEDGE THE LIFE LESSONS..I LEARN FROM THE HISTORY AND I MOVE ON TO GREATER WORKS!!!"

"I PLAN..
I PRAY...
I PREPARE....
I *PRESS...

I PROSPER!!"

*To press is to persevere, meaning to be persistent.

" ALL IS IN DIVINE ORDER...MY RELATIONSHIP WITH MYSELF AND MY GOD"

"I AM RESPONSIBLE FOR WHAT HAPPENS BECAUSE OF ME!!!"

"I WILL FORGIVE MYSELF FOR MY LIFE ERRORS CORRECTING THOSE I CAN AND FORGIVING MYSELF FOR THOSE WHICH CANNOT BE CORRECTED... AND PLACE THEM BEHINID ME!!!"

"I CAN RECOVER FROM ANYTHING BUT DEATH.....ALL THAT HAPPENS TO ME IS AN OPPURTUNITY FOR MY GROWTH!!"

"I HONOR MYSELF IN ALL THAT I DO!!!"

"WHO I AM IS DETERMINED BY CIRCUMSTANCE WHICH I CAN NOW CHANGE!!!!"

"LIFE OFFERS OPTIONS AND

ALTERNATIVES...I

WILL

CHOOSE MY

CONSEQUENCES ...CAREFULLY!!!"

"THERE IS ONLY ONE OF ME..I AM ALWAYS GROWING AND CHANGING...IT IS IMPORTANT TO KNOW WHO I AM!!!"

"I AM NOT AFRIAD TO BE WHO I AM!!"

"I LOVE MYSELF EVEN THOUGH I AM NOT PERFECT!!"

MY JOURNAL
DAY 1

MY JOURNAL
DAY 2

MY JOURNAL
DAY 3

MY JOURNAL
DAY 4

MY JOURNAL
DAY 5

MY JOURNAL
DAY 6

MY JOURNAL
DAY 7

MY JOURNAL
DAY 8

MY JOURNAL
DAY 9

MY JOURNAL
DAY 10

MY JOURNAL
DAY 11

MY JOURNAL
DAY 12

MY JOURNAL
DAY 13

MY JOURNAL
DAY 14

MY JOURNAL
DAY 15

MY JOURNAL
DAY 16

MY JOURNAL
DAY 17

MY JOURNAL
DAY 18

MY JOURNAL
DAY 19

MY JOURNAL
DAY 20

MY JOURNAL
DAY 21

MY JOURNAL
DAY 22

MY JOURNAL
DAY 23

MY JOURNAL
DAY 24

MY JOURNAL
DAY 25

MY JOURNAL
DAY 26

MY JOURNAL
DAY 27

MY JOURNAL
DAY 28

MY JOURNAL
DAY 29

MY JOURNAL
DAY 30

MY JOURNAL
DAY 31

WORLD'S BEST

SELF ACTUALIZER

this certificate is awarded to:

[_____

in recognition of completion
Affirmations for Self Esteem: Affirmations for Conquering Fear in Your Life and
Affirmations of Power

_____   _____
Signature   Date

CONQUERING FEAR IN YOUR LIFE

LIFE SERIES: VOLUME 1
SECTION 2

This is dedicated to my children Chelsea Bailey and Louis Bailey and all the young lives I as a member of the village have touched.

Fear CAN BE CONQUERED. Conquering it is a process. Fear begins in the early stages of our lives. It has sometimes been called our reaction to the unknown or what we perceive we know. My brother Sam once told me a story about why large circus elephants are seemingly restrained with a chain or large rope. He said that the elephant could easily break the chain or the rope. He said that when the elephants were babies the owners put large chains on their legs. The baby elephants fought and pulled against the ropes but the baby elephants were unable to break the chain so the baby elephant learned that when something was put on its leg that it was unbreakable. The baby elephant learned not to even pull at the rope. As the elephant grew the elephant remembered and stopped trying to break the chain. So too in our earlier years we are taught boundaries and we just like the elephant stay within our learned boundaries.

The first step to overcoming fear is naming it. Once it has been named, fear can be relegated to its proper place. Once placed in its proper place then fear can be managed and finally overcome.

"IF YOU GO AS FAR AS YOU CAN INTO FEAR YOU WILL REACH THE OTHER SIDE!!!"

"FEAR IS A TWO SIDED COIN..ONE SIDE IS FEAR THE OTHER SIDE IS GROWTH!!"

"Fear is afraid of movement!!!"

"Fear is rejection in the wrong direction!!"

"fear vanishes in the face of love!!"

"Fear can be unlearned!!"

"I AM A ONE PERSON ARMY..I CAN CONQUER FEAR!!"

"FORGET EARLIER APPLICATIONS OF REJECTION FORGET EARLIER ACTS OF REJECTION!!"

"FEAR IS A MANAGEABLE RESOURCE.......... WHEN USED PROPERLY FEAR WILL BECOME AN ENERGIZER!!"

"I WILL NOT ALLOW FEAR TO INTERFERE WITH MY INTUITIVE PROCESS!!"

"TIME AND THINKING ARE THE GREATEST ENEMIES OF FEAR!!"

"I CAN *CHALLENGE* AND DEFEAT FEAR!!"

"THERE ARE THREE PHASES OF FEAR..THE BEGINNING... THE MIDDLE... THE END!!"

"FEAR IS NOT MY FRIEND... AND I WILL NOT LISTEN TO FEAR!!"

"FEAR PRODUCES ENERGY……………. KNOWLEDGE PRODUCES GROWTH!!"

"FEAR IS IRRATIONAL AND DISAPPEARS IN THE FACE OF LOGIC!!"

"FEAR IS INTERNAL AND EXTERNAL AND SEEKS TO ELUDE DEFINITION!!"

"FEAR DISGUISES ITSELF AS MANY THINGS!!"

"TODAY I WILL NOT FEAR.. I WILL RECOGNIZE THE FEAR AND TAKE ACTION TO DEFEAT IT!!"

"TODAY I WILL SHINE A LIGHT UPON MY FEAR AND DEFEAT IT!!"

AFFIRMATION #21

"I RECOGNIZE FEAR.. I ACKNOWLEDGE FEAR AND I CONQUER FEAR!!"

"MY GOOD SELF ESTEEM WILL DISSOLVE MY FEAR!!"

"THERE IS NOTHING TO FEAR...BUT THE FEAR OF FEAR!!"

FROZEN
ENERGY
ALLEVIATES
REALITY

FEARLESS

ENERGY

ACTIVATES

RESOURCES

AFFIRMATION #26

"FEAR IS MY ENEMY I GIVE IT A FACE!!"

"I WILL SPEAK TO FEAR IN A LOUD VOICE!!"

"I WILL NAME MY FEARS AND PUT THEM AWAY FROM ME!!",

"I WILL NOT LOOK BACK ON MY FEAR!!"

"I AM FEARLESS AND PREPARED FOR SUCCESS!!",

"FEAR WILL NEVER BE A FACTOR IN MY SUCCESS!!"

MY JOURNAL
DAY 1

MY JOURNAL
DAY 2

MY JOURNAL
DAY 3

MY JOURNAL
DAY 4

MY JOURNAL
DAY 5

MY JOURNAL
DAY 6

MY JOURNAL
DAY 7

MY JOURNAL
DAY 8

MY JOURNAL
DAY 9

MY JOURNAL
DAY 10

MY JOURNAL
DAY 11

MY JOURNAL
DAY 12

MY JOURNAL
DAY 13

MY JOURNAL
DAY 14

MY JOURNAL
DAY 15

MY JOURNAL
DAY 16

MY JOURNAL
DAY 17

MY JOURNAL
DAY 18

MY JOURNAL
DAY 19

MY JOURNAL
DAY 20

MY JOURNAL
DAY 21

MY JOURNAL
DAY 22

MY JOURNAL
DAY 23

MY JOURNAL
DAY 24

MY JOURNAL
DAY 25

MY JOURNAL
DAY 26

MY JOURNAL
DAY 27

MY JOURNAL
DAY 28

MY JOURNAL
DAY 29

MY JOURNAL
DAY 30

MY JOURNAL
DAY 31

WORLD'S BEST

SELF ACTUALIZER

this certificate is awarded to:

[_____

in recognition of completion
Affirmations for Self Esteem: Affirmations for Conquering Fear in Your Life and
Affirmations of Power

_____   _____
Signature   Date

AFFIRMATIONS FOR DEVELOPMENT OF POWER IN YOUR LIFE

LIFE SERIES: VOLUME 1
Section 3

This manual is dedicated to my mother who honed my spirituality and to my sisters Mary Hudson-Davis and Rovelma Ann Hudson who always told me I was "Special."

Use the affirmations in the same manner that you used the affirmations for self esteem development. Repeat/ recite and write one through four daily only changing the fifth affirmation for the additional daily affirmations.

Do your self affirming activities each day.

Write daily in your journal. By now journaling should be a daily part of your l life.

I charge you to commit to this manual and at the end of thirty days your life will be forever changed. You will have accomplished two tasks. You will have defined your concept of your Universal Power and explored your relationship with the Universal Power.

There is a move afoot to grasp onto the elusive spirituality. Our spiritual side cries out and we are compelled to answer the call. The cry may come as an almost physical longing to fill the empty spaces. Those who are unable to fill this longing usually become drug addicts, alcoholics, workaholics, mental patients, self abusers with suicidal ideation.

Those who do heed the calling find themselves imbued with a new sense of connectedness with a Universal Power. In tune with the power of positive thinking, positive attitudes and good mental health.

I merely place before you a process to hone your spiritual side . In the process define your relationship with Good and become closer to the Universal Power.

Before we go down the religion road, please understand that the approach taken in this manual seeks to allow you to formulate who and what your Universal Power might be ,up to and including the naming of that Universal Power.

When we call upon the Universal Power and our voice rings back empty and hollow to our own ears. Be assured that the Universal Power is listening. When all we ask seems meaningless be assured that the Universal Power is working it out. When we feel disconnected from the Universal Power know that the Universal Power is still connected to us. Think about the times when your life was so full ,that tears could not express your thanksgiving and even when you try to explain it words are in vain..

The aural feeling of connectedness with the Universal Power will reassert itself. Then you will know that you are part of it all. That you were created as part and parcel of the grand scheme of things.

"I BELIEVE IN A UNIVERSAL POWER GREATER THAN MYSELF!!"

"THE UNIVERSAL POWER IS UNLIMITED!!"

"I AM ONE WITH THE UNIVERSAL POWER!!"

"MY ONENESS WITH THE UNIVERSAL POWER ALLOWS FOR UNCONDITIONAL LOVE AND ACCEPTANCE!!"

"MY ONENESS WITH THE UNIVERSAL POWER ALLOWS FOR RECIPROCAL UNCONDITIONAL LOVE!!"

"THE UNIVERSAL POWER GIVES VOICE TO THE DESIRES OF MY HEART!!"

"THE UNIVERSAL POWER HAS LAWS TO DIRECT HOW I LIVE AND ACT IN RELATIONSHIP WITH THE UNIVERSAL POWER!!"

"THE UNIVERSAL POWER HAS LAWS TO DIRECT HOW I LIVE AND ACT IN RELATIONSHIP WITH MANKIND!!"

"THE UNIVERSAL POWER DIRECTS THAT PEACE FLOWS NATURALLY THROUGH MY RELATIONSHIPS"

"THE UNIVERSAL POWER WILL NEVER DISCONNECT FROM ME!"

"I HAVE CHOICES IN HOW I CHOOSE TO CONNECT TO THE UNIVERSAL POWER!!"

"THE GIFTS I RECEIVE FROM THE UNIVERSAL POWER

WERE GIVEN TO ME BEFORE I WAS CREATED!!"

"THE UNIVERSAL POWER WITHIN ME ALLOWS ME TO CREATE MIRACLES!!"

"EVERY TIME I FEEL THE SUN, WIND RAIN OR SNOW I AM BEING TOUCHED BY THE UNIVERSAL POWER!!"

"I BASK IN THE GLORY OF THE UNIVERSAL POWER IN NATURE!!"

"THE UNIVERSAL POWER IS A CONDUIT TO GREATNESS!"

"JOY , LOVE AND HAPPINESS ARE NATURAL FRUITS OF THE UNIVERSAL POWER!"

AFFIRMATION #18

"I CAN DEFINE MY RELATIONSHIP WITH THE UNIVERSAL POWER!!"

"I WILL LIVE MY LIFE AS AN EXAMPLE FOR OTHERS!!"

"THE UNIVERSAL POWER HAS A PURPOSE FOR ME!!"

"I AM A PART OF THE UNIVERSAL PLAN!!"

AFFIRMATION #22

"I AM INFUSED WITH AN ENERGETIC SPIRIT!!"

"*I AM POWERFUL BEYOND MEASURE!!*"

AFFIRMATION #24

"THE UNIVERSAL SPIRIT IS LOVE"

"I WILL LOVE EVERYONE AND EVERYTHING ...THAT WHICH I CANNOT LOVE" I WILL TRY TO LOVE!!"

"THE UNIVERSAL POWER EMBODIES WISDOM!!"

"I AM A PARTICIPANT WITH THE UNIVERSAL POWER!!"

"I WILL BE BOLD AND AMBITIOUS. I HAVE NO FEAR. THE UNIVERSAL POWER IS WITH ME ALWAYS!!"

"I WILL HEAR WHEN THE UNIVERSAL POWER SPEAKS TO ME!!

"I WILL SEEK TO KNOW THE WILL OF THE UNIVERSAL POWER!!"

MY JOURNAL
DAY 1

MY JOURNAL
DAY 2

MY JOURNAL
DAY 3

MY JOURNAL
DAY 4

MY JOURNAL
DAY 5

MY JOURNAL
DAY 6

MY JOURNAL
DAY 7

MY JOURNAL
DAY 8

MY JOURNAL
DAY 9

MY JOURNAL
DAY 10

MY JOURNAL
DAY 11

MY JOURNAL
DAY 12

MY JOURNAL
DAY 13

MY JOURNAL
DAY 14

MY JOURNAL
DAY 15

MY JOURNAL
DAY 16

_____
_____
_____
_____
_____
_____
_____
_____
_____
_____
_____
_____
_____
_____
_____
_____
_____
_____
_____
_____
_____
_____
_____
_____
_____

MY JOURNAL
DAY 17

MY JOURNAL
DAY 18

MY JOURNAL
DAY 19

MY JOURNAL
DAY 20

MY JOURNAL
DAY 21

MY JOURNAL
DAY 22

MY JOURNAL
DAY 23

MY JOURNAL
DAY 24

MY JOURNAL
DAY 25

MY JOURNAL
DAY 26

MY JOURNAL
DAY 27

MY JOURNAL
DAY 28

MY JOURNAL
DAY 29

MY JOURNAL
DAY 30

MY JOURNAL
DAY 31

WORLD'S BEST

SELF ACTUALIZER

this certificate is awarded to:

[_____

in recognition of completion
Affirmations for Self Esteem: Affirmations for Conquering Fear in Your Life and
Affirmations of Power

_____   _____
Signature   Date

"Nora Hudson, a practicing attorney, counselor and minister believes that sucessful iindividuals have developed truths in their life. These truths if not developed can and must be developed to allow for the utmost growth of the individual. She has dedicated her life to helping others whether it be in her sorority, Delta Sigma Theta Sorority,Inc or whether it be in her law practice. She says we are all inteconnected and our obligation is to "Love One Another". She is the mother of two children, Chelsea and Louis Bailey."

"AFFIRMATIONS FOR SELF ESTEEM DEVELOPMENT, LIFE SERIES: VOLUME 1 contains three volumes-Volume 1: Affirmations for Self Esteem Development, Volume 2 Conquering Fear,Volume 3. Affirmations for Developing Power in your Life. Each Volume stands alone as a method for improving our relationship with ourselves and others."